I didn't know that

some

boats

have

wings

Produced by
Aladdin Books Ltd
28 Percy Street
London W1P 0LD

*First published in the United States
in 1998 by*
Copper Beech Books,
an imprint of
The Millbrook Press
2 Old New Milford Road
Brookfield, Connecticut 06804

Concept, editorial, and design by
David West Children's Books
Illustrators: Ross Watton, Jo Moore

Printed in Belgium
All Rights Reserved
5 4 3 2 1

Library of Congress Cataloging-in-Publication Data
Oliver, Clare.
Some boats have wings : and other amazing facts about ships and
submarines / by Clare Oliver ; illustrated by Ross Watton and Jo Moore.
p. cm. — (I didn't know that)
Summary: Explores early navigation and shipbuilding and surveys the
development of boats from Greek rowboats to the cruise ships of today.
ISBN 0-7613-0736-2 (trade:hc) — ISBN 0-7613-0817-2 (lib. bdg.)
1. Ships—Juvenile literature. 2. Submarines (Ships)—Juvenile literature.
[1. Ships.] I. Watton, Ross, ill. II. Moore, Jo, ill. III. Title. IV. Series.
VM150. 044 1998   98-6803
623.8'2—dc21   CIP AC

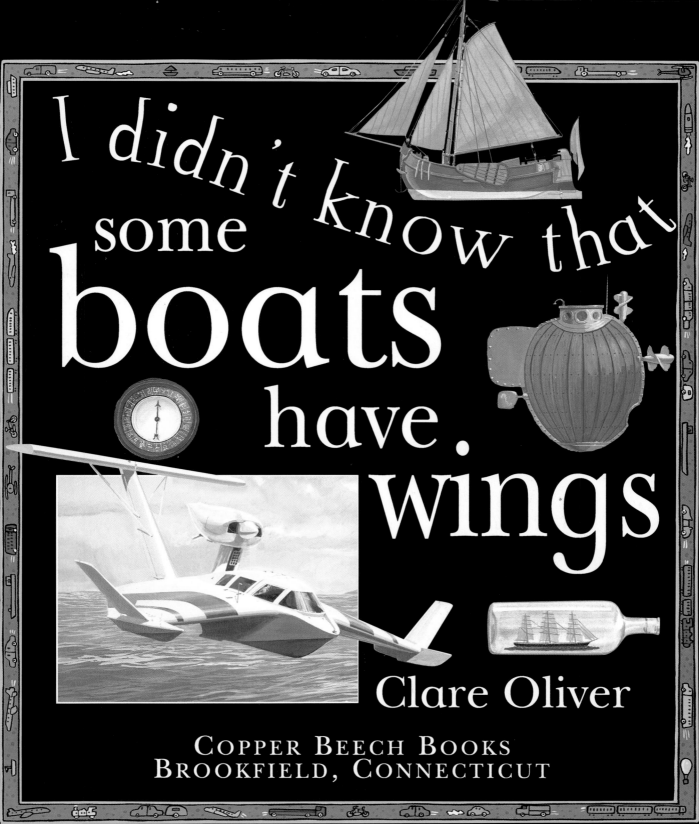

I didn't know that

some

boats

have

wings

Clare Oliver

COPPER BEECH BOOKS
BROOKFIELD, CONNECTICUT

I didn't know that

Introduction

Did *you* know that the first warships were dugout logs? ... that supertankers weigh as much as 1,000 jumbo jets? ... that some boats can fly?

Discover for yourself amazing facts about boats, ships, and submarines. From the earliest rafts to the massive cruise ships that carry nearly 4,000 passengers.

Watch for this symbol that means there is a fun project for you to try.

Is it true or is it false? Watch for this symbol and try to answer the question before reading on for the answer.

Don't forget to check the borders for extra amazing facts.

I didn't know that

the first boats were made of "paper." The ancient Egyptians were making rafts almost 5,000 years ago. They tied together bundles of papyrus reeds, which grew on the banks of the Nile River, and were light enough to float. These reeds were useful for making other things, too, such as ropes and the very first sheets of paper.

SEARCH & FIND & FIND & SEARCH & FIND & SEARCH

Can you find the three hippos?

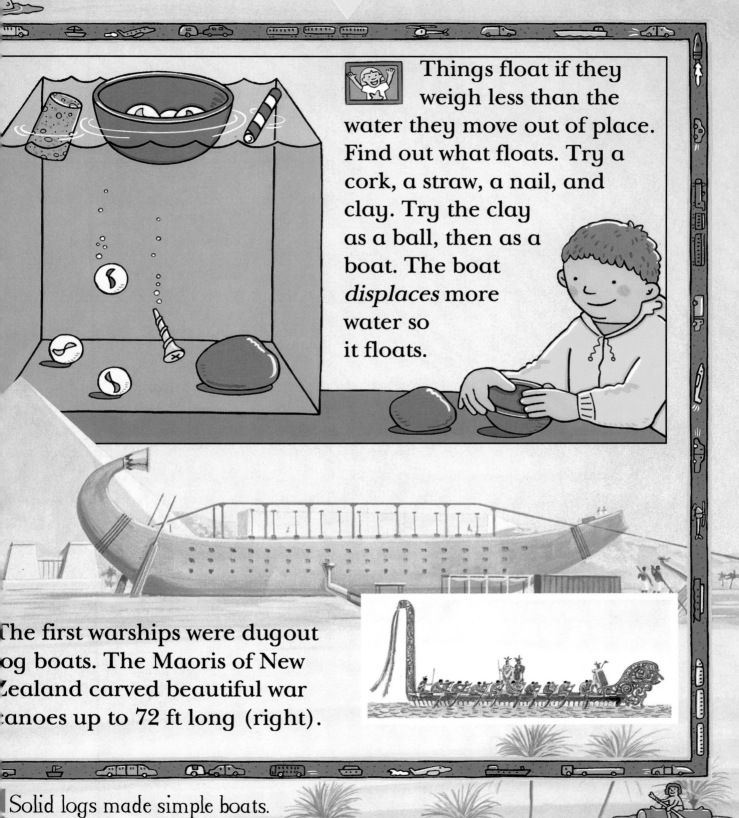

Things float if they weigh less than the water they move out of place. Find out what floats. Try a cork, a straw, a nail, and clay. Try the clay as a ball, then as a boat. The boat *displaces* more water so it floats.

The first warships were dugout log boats. The Maoris of New Zealand carved beautiful war canoes up to 72 ft long (right).

Solid logs made simple boats.

I didn't know that

it took 170 Greeks to row a boat. On the open sea, sails powered Greek warships. The trireme's men saved their strength for battle. Then they rowed at top speed into the enemy. The bronze battering ram on the bow could punch a hole in the enemy's ship to sink her.

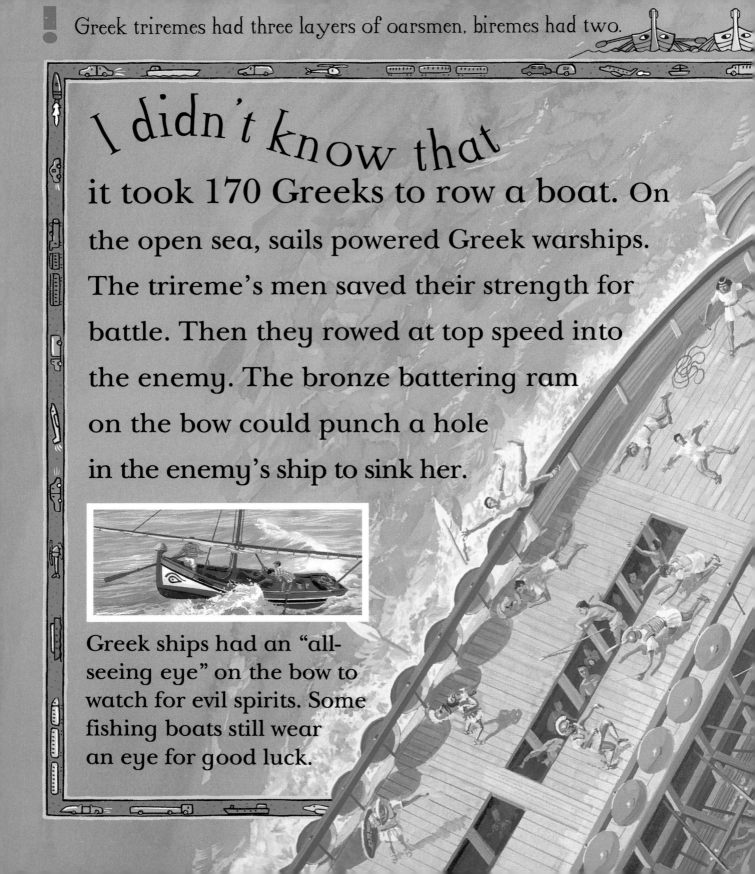

Greek ships had an "all-seeing eye" on the bow to watch for evil spirits. Some fishing boats still wear an eye for good luck.

An oar at the *stern* steered this Indian state barge. It had eight oarsmen each side. The Maharaja sat at the bow.

SEARCH & FIND & SEARCH & FIND

Can you find the flute player?

Today, the most famous "eights" are from Yale and Harvard Universities. The coxswain sits at the stern and shouts directions to the rowers.

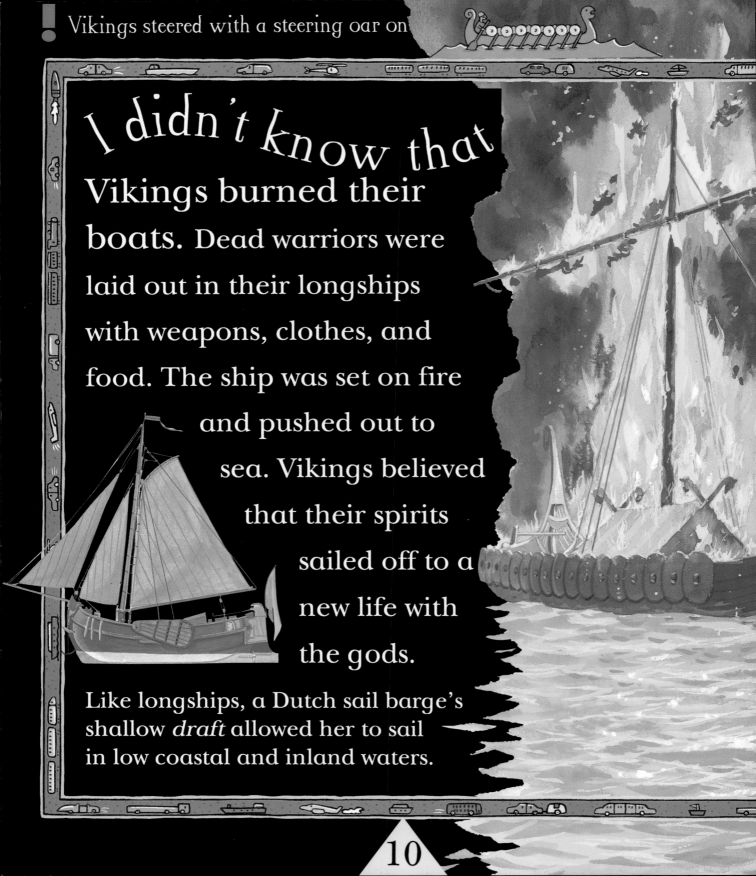

I didn't know that

Vikings burned their boats. Dead warriors were laid out in their longships with weapons, clothes, and food. The ship was set on fire and pushed out to sea. Vikings believed that their spirits sailed off to a new life with the gods.

Like longships, a Dutch sail barge's shallow *draft* allowed her to sail in low coastal and inland waters.

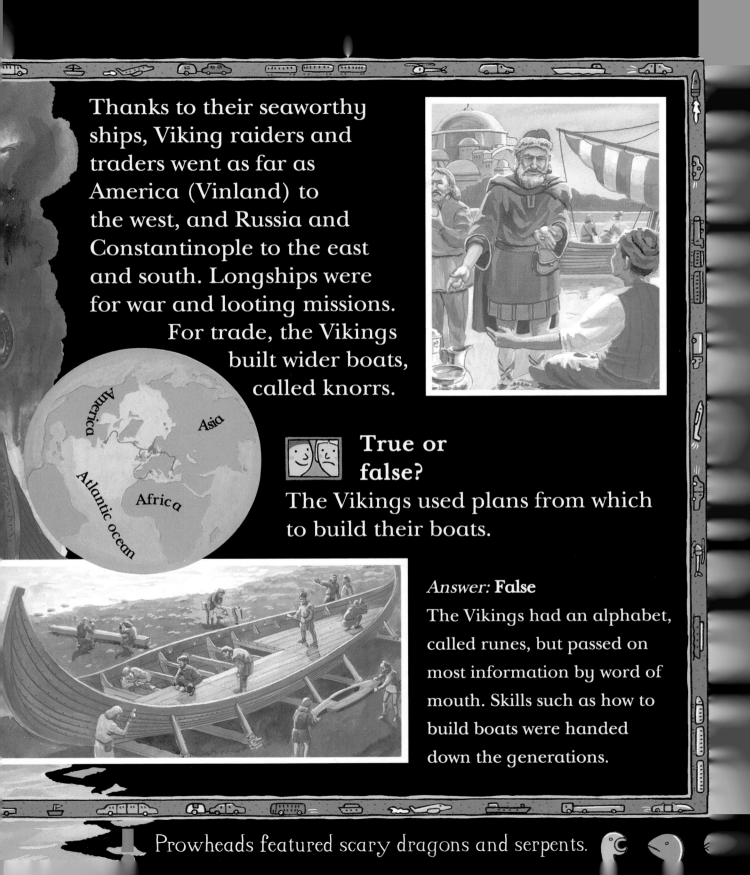

Thanks to their seaworthy ships, Viking raiders and traders went as far as America (Vinland) to the west, and Russia and Constantinople to the east and south. Longships were for war and looting missions. For trade, the Vikings built wider boats, called knorrs.

America

Asia

Atlantic ocean

Africa

True or false?

The Vikings used plans from which to build their boats.

Answer: **False**

The Vikings had an alphabet, called runes, but passed on most information by word of mouth. Skills such as how to build boats were handed down the generations.

Prowheads featured scary dragons and serpents.

I didn't know that

ships found a New World.

In the 1400s, explorers set sail in ships called caravels. Christopher Columbus, looking for a route to India, found America. He called the islands he came to the West Indies.

An astrolabe measured the height and positio of the sun and stars. Using this sailors could chart their position at sea.

12

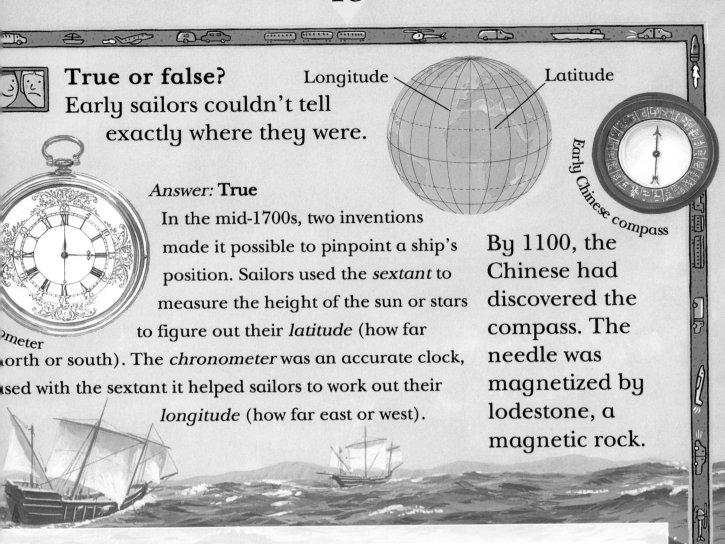

True or false?
Early sailors couldn't tell exactly where they were.

Longitude

Latitude

Early Chinese compass

Answer: **True**

In the mid-1700s, two inventions made it possible to pinpoint a ship's position. Sailors used the *sextant* to measure the height of the sun or stars to figure out their *latitude* (how far north or south). The *chronometer* was an accurate clock, used with the sextant it helped sailors to work out their *longitude* (how far east or west).

ometer

By 1100, the Chinese had discovered the compass. The needle was magnetized by lodestone, a magnetic rock.

The *Mayflower* (right) sailed from England to America in 1620. The families on board wanted a new life in the New World, because they weren't happy with the English king.

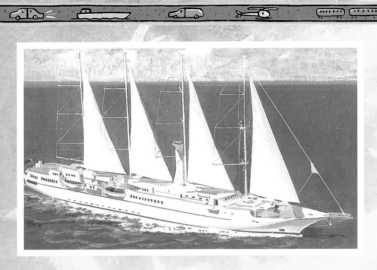

Some modern liners (left) are returning to sail power. They can turn off their engines on ocean voyages to cut down on fuel and pollution.

Yachts are sailing ships used for pleasure and racing. The world's most famous sailboat competition is the America's Cup.

SEARCH & FIND & SEARCH & FIND
Can you find two seagulls?

True or false?
A ship's speed is measured in knots.

Answer: **True**
One knot equals one nautical mile. Early explorers tied a float to a rope with evenly spaced knots. They would throw the float into the sea and count how many knots unraveled into the sea in the time it took an hourglass to empty

Clippers could beat steamships - if the winds were good!

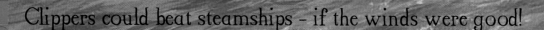

The *Cutty Sark*'s figurehead wore a cutty sark (linen shirt).

I didn't know that

ships sailed on air. With the wind in her sails, a clipper such as the *Cutty Sark* could travel along at 17 knots on air-power alone. This merchant ship had 34 sails and could get a cargo of tea from China to London in 110 days.

This clipper's narrow *hull* (above) could slide through a bottle neck. The hinged mast and sails were pulled up with a wire.

15

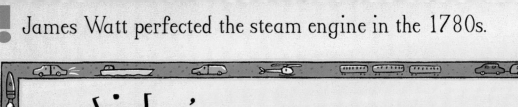

I didn't know that

some ships have wheels. The first steamships used steam power to drive paddle wheels. As the wheels turn, the paddles push against the water and power the boat. Paddle steamers work well in wide, shallow rivers and are used as casinos on the Mississippi River.

SEARCH & FIND

Can you find the gambler?

FIND & SEARCH

The first pedal-powered pleasure boats appeared in the 1800s. Even Queen Victoria had one!

Isambard Brunel's *Great Eastern* didn't take any chances. This steamship, launched in 1858, was driven by sails, paddle wheels, and a *propeller*!

True or false?
Propellers are more powerful than paddles.

Answer: **True**
After the propeller was invented, a tug-of-war was held in 1845 to discover which was best – paddle wheels or propellers? The propeller-powered *Rattler* outpulled the paddle-driven *Alecto*.

True or false?

You could be forced to join the Navy.

Answer: **True**

The low pay, appalling conditions, and long service made going to sea unpopular. So navies used Press Gangs. They were groups of tough sailors who kidnapped men and forced them onto the ships.

Ironclads (right) were the first ships to wear armor. The first battle between ironclads took place in 1862 during the U.S. Civil War. Neither the *Monitor* nor the *Merrimack* came out a clear winner.

The American ship *USS Constitution* had a copper bottom! The metal protected the hull from wood-eating shellfish. It also stopped weeds from growing there thus reducing the boat's *drag* in the water.

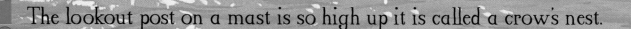
The lookout post on a mast is so high up it is called a crow's nest.

I didn't know that

some warships are made of plastic. Engine noise or a hull's magnetic pull can set off mines. Minesweepers clear underwater bombs (mines). They have silent engines and some have plastic, non-magnetic hulls.

SEARCH & FIND

Can you find the mine?

HMS Middleton
(a "Hunt" class, plastic-hulled minesweeper)

M34

I didn't know that

you can swim on a ship. *Carnival Destiny*, a Caribbean cruise ship, has four swimming pools on board! One pool has a slide 213 ft above sea level and another has a glass roof that slides open.

Most huge liners rely on tugboats and pilots to pull and steer them carefully into the dock. Not the *Destiny*! She can be docked using a joystick in the control room.

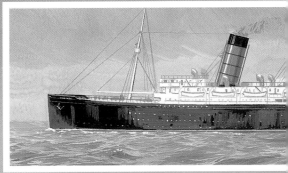

It took an ocean liner just five days to cross the Atlantic Ocean.

Fast, cheap jumbo jets took over from the luxury liners.

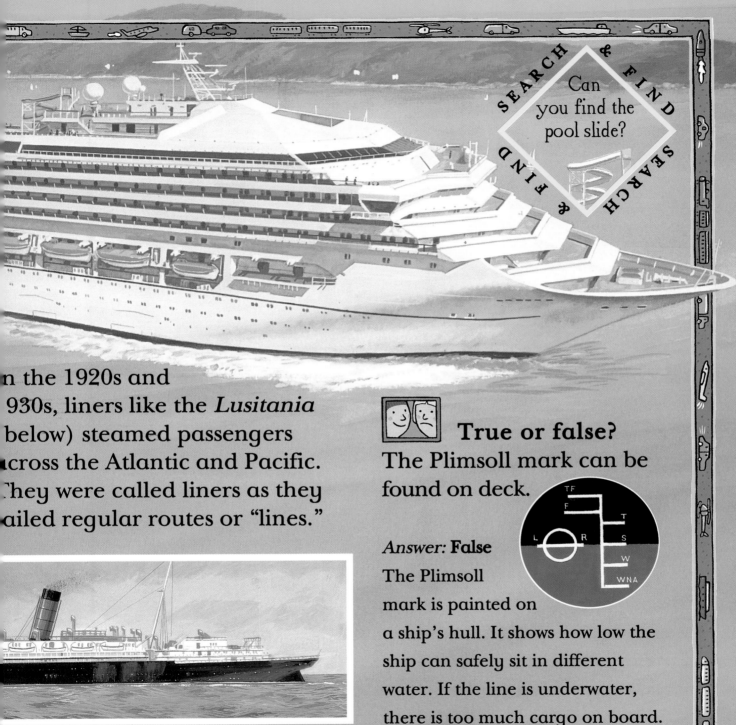

SEARCH & FIND
Can you find the pool slide?
FIND & SEARCH

In the 1920s and 1930s, liners like the *Lusitania* (below) steamed passengers across the Atlantic and Pacific. They were called liners as they sailed regular routes or "lines."

True or false?
The Plimsoll mark can be found on deck.

Answer: **False**
The Plimsoll mark is painted on a ship's hull. It shows how low the ship can safely sit in different water. If the line is underwater, there is too much cargo on board.

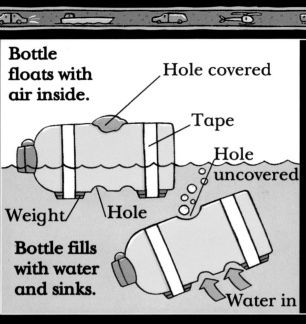

Bottle floats with air inside.

Hole covered

Tape

Hole uncovered

Weight

Hole

Bottle fills with water and sinks.

Water in

Subs have tanks that let water or air in and out so that they can sink or resurface. Ask a grown-up to cut three holes in a plastic bottle. Tape on some weights, like coins. Cover the top hole with clay. The sub will float. Take off the top cover. What happens to the sub?

I didn't know that

Alvin

some boats sink on purpose.

Submarines and submersibles are designed to sink. Submarines are used to sneak up on enemy targets without being seen. Submersibles are much smaller and are used to explore the deep. In 1986, *Alvin* was used to explore the wreck of the *Titanic*, 9,000 ft down on the seabed.

Trieste made the deepest-ever dive – to nearly 36,000 ft.

The *Turtle* was built in 1776. There was room for one person inside, who was kept busy turning the propellers by hand.

The biggest and fastest submarines are the six *nuclear-powered Russian Typhoons* (above). These massive missile machines can top 40 knots. Military submarines cruise the oceans constantly to keep the peace.

Turtle

Titanic

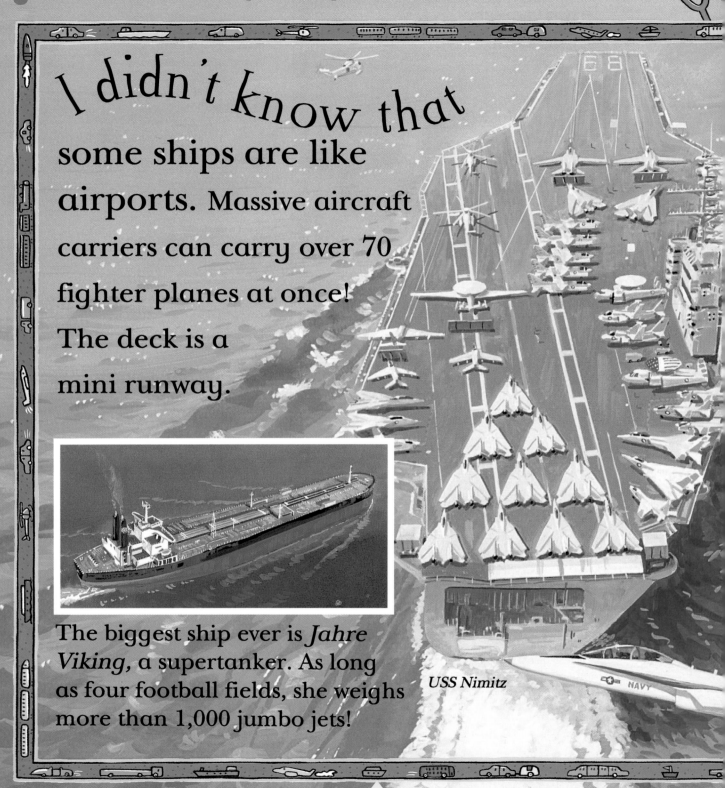

I didn't know that

some ships are like airports. Massive aircraft carriers can carry over 70 fighter planes at once! The deck is a mini runway.

The biggest ship ever is *Jahre Viking,* a supertanker. As long as four football fields, she weighs more than 1,000 jumbo jets!

USS Nimitz

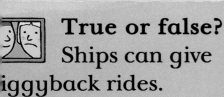

True or false?
Ships can give
piggyback rides.

Answer: **True**

A heavy-lift ship (right) lowers
herself in the water so the smaller
ship can float aboard, then she
rises with the smaller ship on deck.

SEARCH & FIND
Can you find three helicopters?
FIND SEARCH &

An icebreaker (below) cuts
through frozen seas to carve a
path for other ships to follow.

Ships like aircraft carriers,
icebreakers, and some
submarines are nuclear
powered. Nuclear power
allows them to stay at sea
for very long periods
without having to refuel.

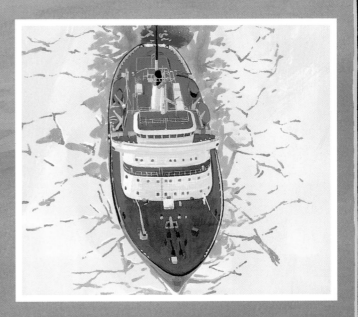

The biggest aircraft carriers need 6,000 people to crew them!

I didn't know that

some boats are unsinkable.

Well, almost! Because lifeboats usually go to sea in dangerous conditions, they can sometimes run into trouble themselves. If a big wave turns the boat over, special *buoyancy tanks* turn the boat the right way up almost immediately.

SEARCH & FIND Can you find the man overboard? SEARCH & FIND

A light ship is like a floating lighthouse with a *beacon* that can be seen from about 24 miles away. She stays anchored in a dangerous spot to warn other ships.

The ocean liner
Titanic (right)
was supposed to be
unsinkable. Disaster
struck when she hit
an iceberg on her
maiden (first)
voyage – and sank.

Some lifeguards
use special rowboats
(right) to patrol the
beaches for swimmers
caught by high waves.

In 1997, Tony Bullimore survived 89 hours inside the hull of his yacht.

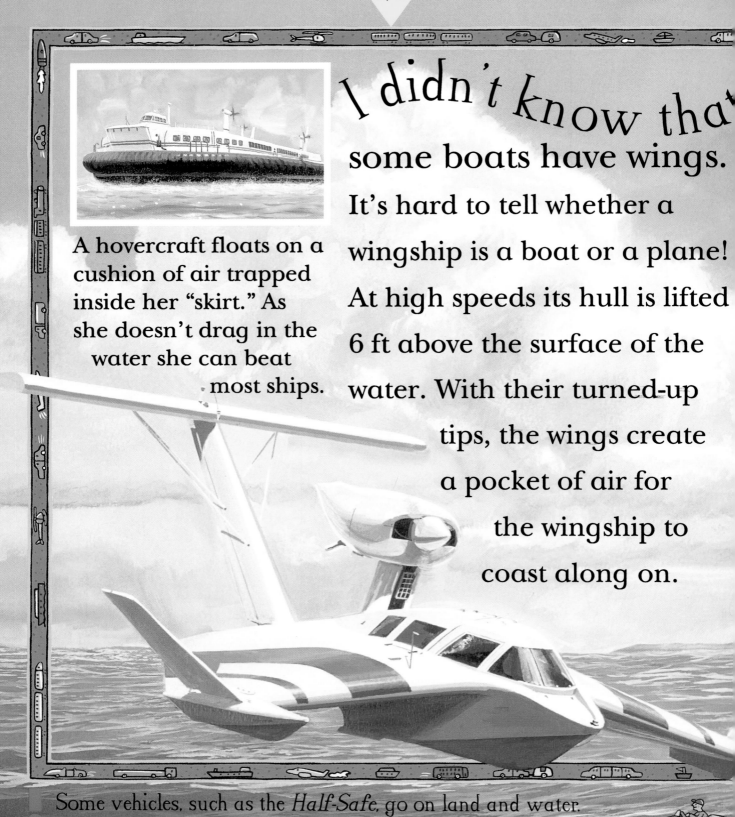

I didn't know that

some boats have wings.

A hovercraft floats on a cushion of air trapped inside her "skirt." As she doesn't drag in the water she can beat most ships.

It's hard to tell whether a wingship is a boat or a plane! At high speeds its hull is lifted 6 ft above the surface of the water. With their turned-up tips, the wings create a pocket of air for the wingship to coast along on.

Some vehicles, such as the *Half-Safe*, go on land and water.

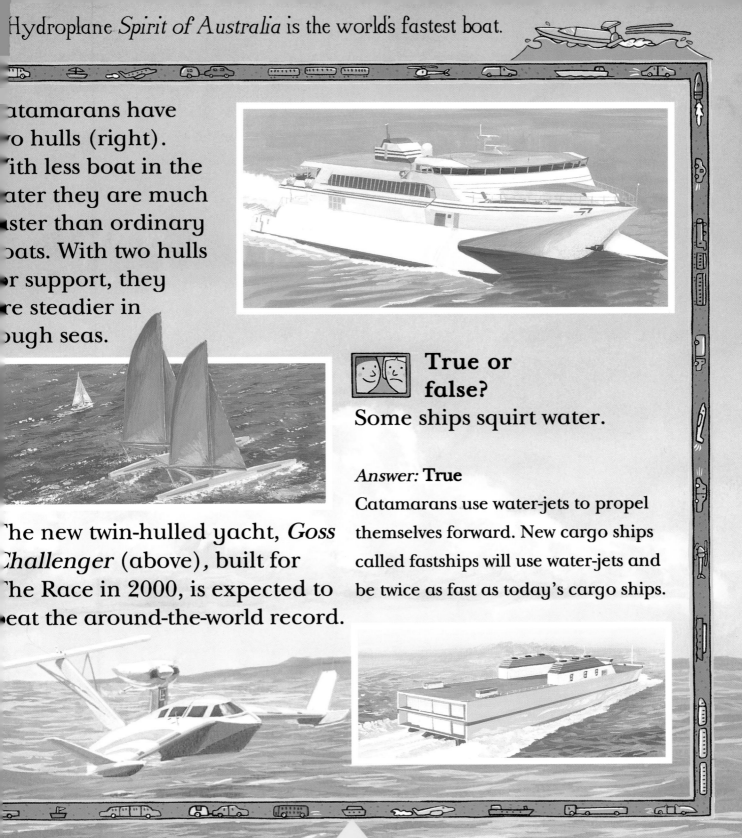

Hydroplane *Spirit of Australia* is the world's fastest boat.

Catamarans have two hulls (right). With less boat in the water they are much faster than ordinary boats. With two hulls for support, they are steadier in rough seas.

The new twin-hulled yacht, *Goss Challenger* (above), built for The Race in 2000, is expected to beat the around-the-world record.

True or false?
Some ships squirt water.

Answer: **True**
Catamarans use water-jets to propel themselves forward. New cargo ships called fastships will use water-jets and be twice as fast as today's cargo ships.

Glossary

Beacon
A strong light to guide ships in dangerous waters.

Buoyancy tanks
Containers that are filled with air. These make lifeboats float very high in the water and stop them from sinking in high seas.

Chronometer
An instrument that lets us figur out longitude by measuring the time accurately.

Displace
To move out of place. The hull of a ship displaces an amount of water equal to the volume of the submerged hull.

Draft
How low a ship sits in the water.

Drag
Water pressing against a boat's hull produces a force called drag that slows the boat down.

Hull
The outer shell of a ship.

Ironclad
Warship of the 19th century that was covered in protective iron plates.

Latitude
Distance north or south of the equator, measured in degrees.

Longitude
Distance east or west of the Greenwich Meridian in London, measured in degrees.

Nuclear power
Some ships travel farther with less fuel by using tiny amounts of powerful radioactive fuels to make steam power.

Propeller
Rotor with angled blades used to propel or push a boat through the water.

Sextant
An instrument that lets us figure out position on the earth's surface by measuring the position of the sun and stars.

Stern
The rear end of a ship.

Index